Discussions with the old Rebbe - Correspondences in dimensions

Gabriel Wayenberg - March 14, 2021

Introduction

This book started with two exchanges. It is the fruit of a long reflection, notably about when exactly would it be acceptable to publish it. I had been thinking about it because of the events that led to it.

Is it not presumptuous to take the pulse of the world and determine when it is the right time? Apparently not. My core audience, the Hasidic leadership, seems to be all focused on that, and they say the equivalent of: when the time is here is the time, from the scriptures.

So there were these exchanges with Rahel from the Orthodox community in Paris, to determine if the topic was relevant. It seems that not only is it relevant, but that it is desirable to address it now, from what I understand, from her point of view.

Obviously, in front of such a subject, it is indispensable to proceed, for the rational soul, to a warning. It is the same for religious souls.

Indeed, this book is a description, through my memories, of the discussions that took place with the old Lubavitch Rebbe, Rav Menachem Shneerson, or the Mashiah for some. There was no oral exchange on this subject. Many of these conversations (all of them, in fact, I believe) were reported to the Chabad by email, 476 in total; that said, often finding a particular conversation on Gmail archived years before is very laborious. Now the space for these conversations spans almost two years - a year and a quarter to be exact, between 2012 and 2013.

Also for religious souls, some will argue that according to the

Talmud one cannot communicate with other worlds, especially with those who have left us. That said, everyone in the Hasidic and religious worlds, and even others, call upon the Tzadikkim (the righteous ones), the most famous of whom is probably Rabbi Nahman of Breslev, whom we simply invoke in everyday life with the formula "Na Nah Nahman hou Meouman". So it depends on who, and also if the communication is requested. In my case, it was the Rebbe who decided to contact me, I did not ask him about it, and this tends to be true for each of the exchanges we had on this subject.

For those in the know, you will understand that this project has some support in the dimensions and that it is important that it be published at an opportune time, in order to be better prepared for the gradual or brutal (I was going to write brittle!) onset of messianic times.

Indeed, many of the Rebbe's teachings, the exchanges in the dimensions have taught me, are extremely useful in the troubled times we live in to find logic and direction to our behavior, to be able to interpret reality and recent events with correct interpretation, with the required wisdom. It is a support for decisions.

This, indeed, one must be able to say it, and to assume it. This is one of the reasons why this book was not published earlier, nor written, at the risk of suffering from fuzzy memories.

It's a bit like my short film "Psychotropic Enthroception", one of my films including a sequence of a Cohen's daughter (from a mixed couple but converted to Judaism) meditating, made me realize that, first of all, this content is not easy to receive for anyone. And also that it can, or could, be misreceived and misinterpreted (Shas ve Shalom, as we say to ward off fate).

But also that it is important to feel when such content, if the patience to present it at the right time is present, can be received in the "least bad" way possible.

Indeed, in my filmic career, it can be argued about my ability to generate a fictional scenario. For me, reality often prevails, hence my production of a docu-fiction or reality fiction aspect. For the more rational among us, this is to be tied to my content, whatever it may be. We will see that the Rebbe approaches this subject with precepts that are precise enough to enlighten our era from a particular and innovative point of view.

The events leading up to the catastrophe at Meron (during Lag'BOmer, April 2021) influenced the writing of a chapter in this book. Indeed, having been interrupted in my writing, a passage had been left open with the last passage sounding like a warning, and I had confused the months (a big mistake) of LagB'Omer, putting it back in Av, the month of tragedy and repentance for the Jewish people.

This had made me just after stopping writing, ask myself questions about the reasons for this sudden stop, and a burst of creativity, as I also suddenly published 7 books of poetry, and made a new short film in the space of 2 days, then promo it to 30.000 views, in French about poetry.

I tried to understand what I perceived because there was a singularity, or rather at this preliminary stage an event convergence that made me call for help outside to try to understand what nature and what type of decree it was going about.

Unfortunately my question was not answered and the drama unfolded.

I am also at the same time writing a paper commissioned by Princeton University, whose theory explains that when one becomes aware of an established singularity in the future, it is possible to put in place avoidance measures, which may turn out to be unconventional, to avoid the worst. I was interested in global warming and the collapse of biodiversity, initially as potential dangers.

Far be it from me to think that Meron's event convergence would land on my radar, but it sure seems like it did.

Then has followed a surgical work of tracing the eventual convergences that I could have thought of, to support the theory.

If we succeed, we will be able to establish a "PreCog" system, i.e. a pre-cognitive system, on which all my work in Israel during this period was based, notably the foundation by testing, and initially by spoofing of a time police unit, the first in the world.

I invite you to discover all this in this book, which is certainly spiritual but not religious in itself, but the precepts discussed are directly derived from Judaic thought.

CHAPTER 1: BACKGROUND

My name in Europe is François, I am the CEO of a Hi-Tech startup that is starting its commercial activities at the time of writing this book. In Israel and as an author, filmmaker and poet, I am Gabriel.

As a consequence of my European function, I write a lot of project funding and presentation documents related to my venture in the olfactory and gustatory field, Ajinomatrix.org. I noticed that it is a professional distortion for me to write the content of this book in a similar way. File presentation, book: "does it pass? " Eventually, you may see the spirit.

Israel, I must remind you, is a path, a Kala ((promised land), a revelation of love, a dream to be fulfilled, and a permanent project through all my projects. However, I am currently writing from Belgium, at the border between different language boundaries, during what seems to be the end of the second containment against COVID, before, during and after the first Pfizer vaccination.

I received my invitation to be vaccinated in Israel in Jerusalem in March, my city, and was waiting for the invitation to be vaccinated here in Rebecq, in Brabant Wallon in Belgium, about 20km from Brussels. I registered on a vaccination platform, but nothing came, and I am a patient at risk in at least 3 factors... Finally the answer arrived, got vaccinated and I am now safer.

Let's get back to Israel.

I made exploratory trips to Israel before I became an Israeli citizen, in order to determine whether I really wanted to live there, and, as explained in my other auto-biographical works, one of these exploratory trips lasted 1 and 3/4 years. This initiative trip is the one we explore in this book.

As I was not yet a national, and as I am bipolar and had interrupted my treatment at the time, I found myself engaged in a whole series of mystical missions, more or less official, due to (or allowed by) my non-stabilisation by my medical treatment.

First of all, I did internships in the Israeli army, Tsahal, and understood that I could continue my military mission afterwards, with a delicate permanent negotiation of my status with the Israeli authorities during my identity checks: I was dressed as a paramilitary and had a few "sponsored" units, some of them very prestigious, which allowed me to stay as long as I did in Eretz (editor's note: in Israel), on a "Tayar" visa (tourist visa)

Honestly, "don't try this at home". Perilous. But it worked. Hats off to Israel: I finally went home only when I expressly reported the request to the authorities, once my mission accomplished (and my condition not allowing me to continue, all in sync – like it must be the case there).

Until I did, I was allowed to proceed with my "mission" by checking in regularly through more or less severe ID checks, "to see if everything was okay," but I was mostly "left alone."

I will not go into detail about these missions, since that is not the purpose of this book at all; it focuses on the one dedicated specifically to the Chabad and the Lubavitcher Rebbe, and our exchanges across dimensions, but I will touch conceptually on some of them making sense in this context.

For a few details are important to highlight the level of spiritual astringency to which I have been and have submitted myself ever since.

For a whole period I was trained by the special forces units in particular, to live in a tolerance in a park outside, in winter (the winters in Jerusalem, which is in altitude, are harsh), in Moshavat Germanit, cohabiting with the "master of the bees", on nearby properties, a dear sweet nut.

Park where I was allowed to set up a Bear Grylls-like camp (see "Ultimate Survival", Discovery Channel), while living on a budget of less than $550 per month and making the system work. This is quite possible in Jerusalem.

In addition, for one of my missions, I needed a new iPhone 5, which I managed to acquire under these conditions with my budget, and without which I would not have been able to transmit all those reports that I managed to transmit at the time. Including the ones I transmitted to the Chabad about discussions with the Rebbe, usually from the old city. Thanks to the free wifi. Thanks G-d!

On my way to Mea Shearim, the children would run up beside me on my way to the Toldos Avrom-Yitzhok synagogue and eagerly ask me, "Atah Hayal? "(Are you a soldier?) - to which I would invariably reply, "Lo, ani Commander! "(No, I am in command!).

This is the best way to start a deaf dialogue among the Haredim.

For them, I was one of those court curiosities (Hasidic congregations generally take this form of organization, like a royal court - there is always a fool - that I was or am, for you to choose), and regularly presented the progress of my work (Avodat Hashem) to the Rabbi of the above mentioned congregation, along with the other Bahurim (young Bar-Mitzvahs of the congregation), accepted in and in line with them (the congregation in general).

Such was the rather good-natured context of these missions.

I was allowed to reconcile military and spiritual missions with total freedom of action. I was truly blessed with exceptional luck and support from all sides, once the seriousness of my mission was established and the inexorability of my motivation was verified. You will see how this all unfolded in the next few chapters.

CHAPTER 2: WHAT I REMEMBER - THE JERUSALEM TOUR

At the time of my outdoor camp, and before that as well, my life was punctuated by the life of resourcefulness but also the very active (and intense!) spiritual life in Jerusalem.

I would get up in my park in Moshavat Germanit at sunrise, with a beautiful view of the valley. I lived in a kind of self-build Sukkah (hut), very discreet in a corner of the landscaped park, at the foot of a tree. I was awakened by the birds, took my canteen and did my morning ablutions. I would go to the public park located one street up, and there I would get ready for the day, personal cleansing, etc. If it was not available I would go to Tahanat Rishona, a secular place where there was a new toilet just freshly built.

Then I went to the local synagogue, located on the street that goes down from the Belgian consulate, located on the roudnabout above. There, I would do the morning prayer and eat at the brunch buffet provided for this time of day. Then I went further to the first Habad synagogue in the area, near another small park, a "square".

From there my route was well codified, I went through an orthodox neighborhood with several synas that I sometimes frequented if I had things to do. Finally, I passed the small key and cobbler store and then the Japanese sushi restaurant, on my way from the Mahane Yehuda Shouk to Agripas.

Or I would go to the old city from Tahanat Rishona, and walk up the small path that you can see from the Jerusalem media library. There I would sit and have coffee with my Chabad friends from the Tsemar Tsedek and at the same time do them some security services, just by being present with my paramilitary uniform; the room was always occupied by myself in the morning.

It was there, essentially, that under a well-known portrait of the Rebbe, the one that gives you the impression of being watched by his gaze at every place you stand around in the room by him, that I wrote the messages.

I didn't have a digital subscription, just an open international line from my Belgian number, so once I had written the messages, I had to go to a free wifi dome to send them from there.

I was once followed by a Bahur who lived in one of the buildings where the wifi was presumably coming from; he seemed to understand what I was doing and started following me. He looked disgruntled. I passed by the East Jerusalem Shuk that day, and there was an altercation on the way – an Arab who was aranguing the YamRams (border patrol).

I had to go somewhere by streetcar with the Rakevet Kala (light rail) that I had to take at the exit of the Shuk below the Vatican building, and I remember that it stopped following me that before entering the Arab part of the Shuk, just after the altercation.

He looked very unhappy. But he didn't want to hear my explanations, nor could we really understand each other because my Hebrew was still in its infancy, and his English even more so...

Apart from this episode, nothing has ever gone wrong in the old town. Except maybe, one day a tour guide had gotten angry at me, but that was only a minor incident. We had had an argument about the possible upcoming construction of the third temple. He didn't like one of my arguments and pretended to sue me, which ended as quickly as it began, that is, with the return of calm to the old city.

In short.

Then I would leave from the Chabad center of Tsemar Tsedek to the free restaurant, either the one at the Kotel or the canteen at Meah Shearim.

I usually returned in the afternoon either to Tsemat Tzedek and back to Mea Shearim and in the evening attended a Shiur at the Tabernacle next to the Toldos Avrom Yitzrok one of the large synagogues in Mea Shearim, and then returned all the way along the old city wall to my camp, at sunset or relatively soon after in winter.

CHAPTER 3 : MY ILLNESS AND THE PARTAGE OF THINGS

As I explained in the introduction, it is important to clarify that during this period, as a bipolar, I arrived stabilized in Israel with an effective medication, but that, under my (medically misguided) initiative, I decided to experiment with stopping taking it to see what experience Israel would hold for me (if you are bipolar, never try to stop taking your medication, please. Its very dangerous).

I did it with confidence, because I know I was going to be treated well, and humanely. I have been at every identity check, and every time I have explained clearly what I was doing, and provided that English was understood, it has been a good experience every time, even if I have been detained sometimes up to a few hours, the time to verify my statements with the hierarchy and for the authorities to make a decision.

Indeed, the state of Israel has a habit of using people suffering from a disability in the army, and in my version of the illness, not supported by the treatment (which I could only allow myself once in a lifetime, because of the important risks of decompensation incurred), I experience several phases over a period of about a year and a half: a manic phase – where I am capable of things that I definitely cannot do in my normal stabilized state (sharp intelligence, and on the HP side, few hours of sleep) – and a so-called "depressive" phase where I literally recover from my manic phase and enter into lethargic decompensation, sleeping a lot as a consequence.

Having already proved in the past the attractiveness of working in this way, I had succeeded, during a previous phase of my life, in autarky in my farmhouse by the sea in Knokke, Belgium, to get in touch with NASA and to realize several collaborative works as an "independent surveyor".

So I had my back against the wall with my good resolutions and my mission could begin.

The first one I set out to do was to conduct a form of public simulation, a test, of the acceptability of building the third Temple in Jerusalem. Needless to say, this delighted the Rebbe of blessed memory.

The second was suggested to me by the Rebbe himself, through meditative contacts with the great tzaddikim, to transmit his teaching from across the dimensions, to the Chabad and to the Hasidim interested in what he had to say from where he was, through my various adventures.

The third was to conduct exercises at different levels of military command, which to date remains entirely confidential and outside the scope of this book, but some points will nevertheless be addressed when useful to cope with understanding the what and what nots.

It's important to list them as I just did, because depending on the context, this information will have a certain level of meaning.

It seemed to me that a level of symbolism was important to acquire in order to be able to represent my role.

So I shaped a character that would be best equipped for the multiple challenges I would face, as if I knew what was coming.

Without further hesitation, let's get to the heart of the matter.

CHAPTER 4: ON THE REAL INVENTIVENESS OF FANTASY STORYTELLERS AND FICTION IN GENERAL

It is not easy to separate my personal delusion of bipolarity from the reality of the messianic age we are approaching from it. But I have to realize that, because of my ability to write this book in full possession of my abilities - I have now been stabilized for several years, and the thing is that it is possible to find a logic to almost everything.

Initially, I had based myself on a Japanese series, Saint Seya (Les Chevaliers du Zodiaque in French) to get a representation in character integration that would have the spiritual power to face the challenges posed by the situation I was about to confront. It was the way I had found to reassure myself of the magnitude of the mission. Living independently on a budget normally too small for my survival, in an expensive city like Jerusalem, a more expensive than my home city, Brussels, was not an easy task. $550 and basta cozy.

So I chose a character who is able to come back as many times as possible and especially as necessary, and who does it to help his brother. In the series, it is Ikki, the Phoenix Knight, who has a little brother. The interest and the report?

I must say that I had initially detected none, but one of the first contacts in communication with the Rebbe brought me the answer to this question.

The Rebbe explained to me, and asked me to pass on, that when a creator of fiction imagines that he is creating with his pure inventiveness, in fact, he is not fully aware of the process to which he is subjected.

The Rebbe supported his reasoning with the fact that when one creates fantasy out of pure imagination, it is really more of a transference – for in his view, let us not be presumptuous since everything comes from G-d - the Universe being such a vast and complex set of worlds that we cannot imagine its extent.

Therefore, the Rebbe explained to me, probably each of these worlds actually exist. In ways and forms that escape our limited understanding and from which we can only derive a certain form of humanized simplification; nevertheless, from there, according to him, comes the real source of inspiration for these fantastic tales.

It is important to underline here that Israel is one of the most open countries in the world to other civilizations. I remember my Assimil Hebrew learning book, in which there was a sketch of an alien in his saucer greeting an Israeli! What could be more normal! No need to make a big deal out of it...

It is in this context and in a broader vision that the Earth is understood as part of a whole at the level of worlds in the Universe, with allies and enemies, according to the version I was able to grasp while staying in Jerusalem for so long in nature, and that the Earth is a relatively elaborate world at the natural and civilizational level, even if its level of technological maturity is low or low, nevertheless it is a wonderful natural reserve.

In this sense, the information coming from the Rebbe is a real blessing because it allows us to realize how the transmission functions at the level of the imaginary and the dream, can be explained and curiously in a more rational way, through the dimensions.

Obviously at this point what we lack is proof. But, it seems, these are not new issues and date back to the time of King David, or even earlier.

How can we explain this constant advance of the Jewish people, created by an agreement with G-d?

Let's say that there are reasons that are not easily shared with the common people, because, from what I understand, it is not easy to maintain a medium level of respect in the population, if all this information was revealed to Mr. Everybody, it will not be easy to accept, and respect might be lacking.

In other words, our civilization is at or near the point of singularity, but not quite yet, so not quite ready or mature. But certainly it is close.

CHAPTER 5: ON THE IMPORTANCE OF FRENCH SPEAKERS IN THE COMING ERA AND ISRAEL

This part, very inspiring but very conflicting, especially in the orthodox parts of the population, is simply the simple interpretation of the phonetics of Israel in French and its meaning.

I won't go into the importance and geographical distribution of the use of French throughout history, but this will make you wonder how simple it is.

In French, Israel sounds "Y sera L" which can be rewritten "il sera elle" and opens, contrary to what I frequently see in forums, the possibility - as progressive Judaism wants - for the genders to come closer together alike.

There is already a relative feminization of men as the generations advance. Also in terms of style. At this level, it is also a signal that transgenders are messengers of the times to come.

The complexity of forming their identity is a journey comparable to the complexity of converting to Judaism, and integrating into the new Jewish identity successfully.

I have to say that on such conflicting issues, the Rebbe didn't really dare to step forward, but what I must say is that I learned a lot from exploring the reality of this path. I did not receive a direct reprimand from him, but an incident with the Chabad at the end of the course caused me to be repatriated to Europe on my own initiative, on my own freewill.

Indeed, often having women's clothes laid out for reuse on the low walls of the properties, I experimented with dressing up as a woman - and noticed the immense peculiarity of being dressed up as an orthodox woman, in Jerusalem: you are left in peace! An imperial peace. Really, in Jerusalem at least, I was marked by this fact. I have no experience of having done it elsewhere, it would never have crossed my mind.

Then it was also an initiative that led to another exercise: I wanted to test the disguise of a Cohen in the Temple, to support the exercises I was doing on social networks a series of tests about the feasibility and admissibility of the coming Third Temple; what a surprise that I was accepted quite normally by the Haredim in Meah Shearim. I think they noticed that I was going out of my way and accepted the "hardship" of having the "hutzpah" to walk around the Orthodox neighborhood like that. I did it. Good experience.

The repatriation to Europe was done for an unfortunate reason: a tolerance allowed me to enter the canteen of a synagogue at night. As sometimes the days were very rainy and I had to dry a few things there so as not to lose them to mold. One evening, the Bahurim of the Yeshiva above the synagogue thought it best to lock the front door, and I tried to intercede for them to open it. Of course, they got angry and locked the door in a spirit of contradiction.

Finally, what was supposed to happen happened: I stepped in the door and the weak lock went on the floor. Technically my immediate problem was solved, it was silly, but legally I had committed a break-in.

Some time later, the director of the Yeshiva decided to report me. And gave me the opportunity to go back to Europe for treatment and to manage my affairs. But that's another story!
Let's continue!

CHAPTER 6: THERE IS A LINK BETWEEN THE FORCES OF 4, THE ORDER OF NATIONS AND CLIMATE COLLAPSE

Do you know the interpretative alphabet of the Arabic numbers from 0 to 9? Here it is

1 : unity, to win (won = one), to be

2 : < less than - also (too = two)

3: tree, or a backside, arse (shape of 3)

4 : forces of 4 (mafia, nazis)

5 : speed (S, speed)

6: Sex (six)

7 : > greater than

8 : forces of 8 (sacred)

9: no (nine)

0: alliance, belonging, "integrated with" (set theory)

It seems well established that in the forces playing last resort, there is a need to distort the negativity of the 4 forces and bring them back to 8, when imminent and concerted action is needed, which is often made possible by the alliance with religious forces.

The Rebbe emphasizes this by the fact that there is indeed an awareness of a general derailment and deforestation of the creation that has been offered to man. Therefore, if he does not take proper care of what he has "received" in a logic of 8, it is only natural that he will go down with His gift, that is to say an end due to the collapse of climate and biodiversity.

In this context, the Rabbi advocates an alliance of these forces, which may seem unnatural. In English we speak of "un-foeing" the forces, that is to say, of forming a type of alliance beneficial to the whole of humanity.

Speaking of which, there seems to be a temporary aspect to this state of "Tikkun-Olam" (repairing the world), as if it could only be done in the short term. In reality, and given that the action needed is on the longer term and over a generation span, it is a short term-long term, rather, in terms of generations span.

Why is this so and what did I get out of it today?

Recently, during the year 2020, I started writing a scientific article commissioned by Princeton University, in order to confirm this state of affairs: in fact, I theorize that, once informed of the state of things as of a threatening singularity event to human lives, confronted with the factual state of our situation on Earth, everyone gains a special kind of faculty, a faculty making us capable of getting out of the initiated stagnation and collectively escaping from the inevitable, based on action.

In fact, according to the article, the theory is that everyone on this path of information will gain the ability to participate in a collective action with their own contribution, as well as to participate in avoiding the catastrophe (the disappearance of the human species), consequence of the lack of consideration and care given to the planet we have inherited.

It is now interesting to see what the reaction is to the knowledge of such a theory by the elites and decision-makers: it turns out that it is still an unofficial fact that they do not want to take into account and try to avoid if possible.

It is clear that there is a fundamental problem of Hattikun which is not easily accessible. It is necessary to find out for what reason - what Avera (misconduct) humanity has committed, for not being able to "roughly" have the ability to perceive danger and to act properly as a consequence.

For this, if you follow my reasoning, it is necessary to proceed to an in-depth analysis of the situation, to identify the signs in synchronicity and to perceive for what reason the "access rights" to the Hattikun (repair) of the climate and to the protection of the species, became inaccessible to us.

This is due, I think, to the fact that we live mostly indoors, in our homes, and no longer have our biorhythms in tune with nature, as a form of non-perception. It is by taking an excessive comfort in relation to creation that we are thus "punished", probably, by cutting ourselves off from our natural metabolism. Of the weight of habits...

If we refer to the scriptures, this may be due to some rather intricate episodes, like Moses, who struck the rock with his stick to make water come out of it when he was expected to teach the people how to do so instead, that he would have lost his right to come and immigrate to Israel.

In the same way, it is important to perform a Tikkun in time and get back in touch with nature sufficiently so that in a form of Pessach safeguarding, during the last plague of Egypt (painting the blood lintels of the Passover sacrifice), we earn the right to collective survival as a species on Earth.

It remains to find the symbolic action that would correspond to it. Karmic action.

We can therefore see that the Jewish symbolism of the Messiah is not vain, for the fact that he is human is important because his action is within the reach of all in terms of understanding, or rather we would all have the capacity to understand the nature and justification of his action, at the basis and origin of it.

Then, the fact that nations are able to pour themselves into a peace regime by multiplying their action on a large scale ecological plan is a costly but indispensable restructuring for the success of the plan to save our world.

This is the message and it is clear: "It is through adherence to the ability to dehaitize the forces of 4 that a revival of salvation by the nations of the world will take place in practice. »

CHAPTER 7: THERE SEEM TO BE BIPOLAR JEWISH-CHRISTIAN AND JEWISH-MUSLIM ALLIANCES.

Each one has its own specificity. One is long standing one is birthing.

It is common for Jews to consider the scriptures of Muslims as a gift from the sages of Judaism.

It is common nowadays to talk about a basis for common agreements so that peace exchanges can take place.

In my experience at the time, I bought a Ritter chocolate, and found that the marzipan tasted of alcohol. There followed a long demonstration of whether it was Kosher, whether it was also something that Muslims could consume freely, in their own abidance.

So I wondered what would be required for a daily friendship between Jews and Muslims. As I am generally a great friend of both Christians and Muslims, the question was on my mind and I thought that it would probably require the lowest possible consumption of alcohol.

Of course we have the Kiddush (blessing on the wine), and at this time, drinking it is sacred; as at Pessar, where one must drink 4 glasses, and at Purim, until one no longer knows one's friend from one's enemy. But one can certainly drink grape juice instead... And still perform the blessing.

At that moment, it occurred to me that the minimum consumption of alcohol is the most suitable common denominator, if one wants to adopt impeccable conduct in the 3 monotheistic dimensions. No matter what the aficionados of alcoholic beverages think.

Today, while taking my bipolar medication regularly, I have an induced side effect, which is type 2 diabetes. I consume as little wine and alcohol as possible, as their effect on my blood sugar is disastrous. Speakin of coïncidences... But I wasn't drinking much either before anyway.

Strange conjunction of events. Even if I wanted to, it would be extremely bad for my health.

Another consideration that intrigued me greatly when I later lived in Israel as a citizen with full rights, and already at the time of these initial questions, was the status of Kosher-organic.

Indeed, there is an aspect of Kosher food that is "better" than normal food, which I could detect by tasting it, or at least it gave me that impression. Nevertheless, it is rare for Jews in the Diaspora to have access to both Kosher and organic food at the same time.

I think that being able to eat organic is a right, and that it is very important and beneficial to health. What shocked me in the demonstration related to this Ritter Sport chocolate, is also that Hasidim generally have on average a less fresh and organic access to food than normal, which I find a form of discrimination.

At this level I think do I have the approval of the Rebbe because it is very important that all Jewish communities receive fair and equal treatment, and able to equalize and reflect. Though, remains the question of Purim (Carnival)... There the Jewish people have to drink to some extend.

CHAPTER 8: CHABAD COOPERATED IN ESTABLISHING A TIME POLICE

When I arrived in Israel for this 1 year 3/4 stay, I asked myself how I could face the important mission that awaited me – to order what had not yet been ordered.

It is therefore by maintaining a stable order, that the Chabad and the Hassids have contributed to the order necessary to host and enable one of the most important developments in terms of maintaining order and peace during that time, with great (stealthy?) support from the authorities.

I am no longer able, as I am not in the ascending phase (which makes my IQ take off and brings my EQ to its maximum potential towards 210) of bipolarity (I am a type 2 bipolar and my phase is 1.5 years long), to retrace the initial operations that were carried out - and moreover, being bound by confidentiality – these titles that I used to carry remain unofficial, but I can shed light on terminologies that are found in films such as "Minority Report".

Example: an action can be "precogged", to manifest a particular situation, here in the context of maintaining order and mutual contingencies between Christians and Orthodox Jews of Chabad.

There is a lot to be said about this.

Particularly in terms of following up on what we put together, I can only notice a parallel between "Back to the Future" and its Biff and President Trump.

Indeed, in the context of regulating the forces in place, I can only defer to the incredible exercise of Chesed (generosity) of the United States through the trust in democracy through the Trump presidency, and the maintenance of order following the victory of his rival.

Indeed, everything could make us fear the drift of the presidency towards less democratic situations, like those experienced in Germany, Israel and Russia with long term established leaders.

But what has happened in practice? The "pre-cogging" of what the continuation of Trump's presidency on a second term – despite his many positive contributions for Israel and peace in the Middle East, were considered carefully in relation to the drifts of the American democratic system, which proved to be uncorrupted by the trade-off presented, in the very end.

This interesting demonstration can be seen in Israel at smaller scales and are essential to maintain order at a smaller level when it comes to democracy.

You will have understood that I don't like to go into details or to go into the heart of the matter because this is the confidential part, but I can assure you that these regulatory systems resulting directly from the alliance of the allies during the second world war are still in action and operational, and allow us to maintain democracy and the white forces in place.

As long as this is the case, and it is, one must continue to trust the establishment, which is constituted and regulated correctly most of the time, and if not, the movements and mechanisms of adjustment and regulation exist and are operational in an effective way, through the functioning of institutions and of the many watch-dog organizations within Western societies and within many Asian societies.

I hope that it will be possible to set up the same kind of effective regulation on a climatic level, because on this subject, one cannot yet say that the situation is so rosy; the "odds" are not yet established on the level of our collective faculty to fight the "owner" of the Earth, on a legal basis that is to our advantage at the same time and in consideration of the diversity of nature, a "constitutional" need indispensable to our long term survival.

Framing the problem in this way gives humanity a more mature form of responsibility.

The regulation at this level is not yet on a winning dimension, simply because it is not (yet) established on democratic bases, and the lobbying imposed by the big companies can easily get out of the considerations necessary for the survival of the human species on Earth, more of an oligopoly at the moment.

This must be situated, Israel is not yet an ecological superpower; there is not yet a real reference at this level that can serve as a broad-spectrum example to convince the outside world... It's a bit like the problem of Kosher-Bio. Everything remains to be done. But what is the penetration rate of Kosher-Bio in Israel? That's the question that situates the current problem.

Nevertheless, it is certain that the situation can change very quickly. And it would be super important to be able to make this change in a short-term window of opportunity.

Work is in progress, but there is a lot on the fire...

CHAPTER 9: THE IMPORTANCE OF LOVE IN JUDAISM

One of the last words to appear before the most important prayer in Judaism is Ahava, in the prayer book.

In the reading flow, it is said that this prayer must be done in love, and it is a prayer that determines many things for the Jewish practitioner, when he does it with conviction.

Although human civilization is far from being distinguished solely by its capacity to love, it is nevertheless a primordial part of it.

We see a lot on social networks, of these videos, where, by expression of love and care, the man manages to get closer to many living species, with a level of understanding of them sometimes unexpected or appalling.

The love of this fact exceeds the kinds, the species, and inspires the respect of the nature, with reciprocity.

However, it is sometimes difficult to express these values openly in the Hasidic world, where the animal is rarely integrated into the home. Yet our patriarchs were often in contact with many animals and raised a livestock. Could this be a fallen or forgotten intelligence?

In particular, among the sages, I would mention the Becht (Baal

Shem Tov), for whom respect for animals was very important to implement, and clearly an intelligence in itself.

Indeed, the following passage confirms this:

The Baal Shem Tov (R. Yisrael Ben Eliezer, 1698-1760), founder of the Hasidic movement, says: "Do not consider yourself superior to anyone else. In truth, you are no different from any other creature, since all things were created to serve God. As God bestows consciousness on you, so He bestows consciousness on your fellow creatures. How is a human being superior to an earthworm?
The worm serves the Creator with all its intelligence and abilities; and man too is compared to a worm or maggot, as the verse says: "I am a worm and not a man" (Psalms 22:7). If God had not given you human intelligence, you would only be able to serve Him as a worm. In this sense, you are both equal in the eyes of Heaven. A person should consider himself, the worm and all creatures as comrades in the universe, for we are all created beings whose abilities are given by God..." (Tzava'as HaRivash 12)

(...)

Therefore, the Baal Shem Tov teaches us, the enlightened person will feel the fellowship of "man, worm and all the little creatures", and will relate to all God's works with love. As the Maharal of Prague (R. Yehudah Loewi Ben Betzalel, 1512-1609) observes, "the love of all creatures is also the love of God; for whoever loves the One, loves all the works that He has made" (Nesivos Olam, Ahavas Re'i, 1). The realization of this truth is the central point of Jewish mysticism. And it is the root of the Jewish ethic of compassion for all creatures. (Source: https://www.jewishveg.org/DSrespect.html)

We see that, despite some aspects such as the domestication of animals and the evolution of their behavior in symbiosis with humans or among themselves, is an important indicator of the evolution of nature in the world to come, and an aspect too often neglected.

CHAPTER 10: JERUSALEM, A NEUTRAL SAFE HAVEN FOR MONOTHEISTIC BELIEFS

Jerusalem is an important crossroads of ethnic diversity and beliefs, a major cultural melting pot and a source of solutions for many problems that arose there a long time ago and have been resolved in recent times or even very recently.

This idea of making Jerusalem a "Washington" of beliefs is probably not new... But how delicate a subject!

Either it is said that the Islamic writings do not mention Jerusalem explicitly – or it is said that Al-Aqsa which is mentioned there is another mosque.

What about the Roman Christians who spilled pig's blood on the Temple esplanade?

These realities and especially the Waqf's control over the Temple Mount and its many synonyms (the Esplanade of the Moques,...) and the Muslim architectural domination of this space should not interfere with the Jewish or even Judeo-Christian dream of rebuilding the 3rd Beit Hamikdash, the Third Temple.

I saw these elements clearly in the dimensions. The architecture of the Temple will have to be heliportable because it must be able to arrive from the sky. It's obvious, what we use, cars, are still too heavy. We are moving towards air-grade. Elon Musk wants his new roadster (at the time of this writing) to "make little hops, from one strip to another", while flying.

This requires much lighter materials and architecture, including what will be used for the construction of the temple. The efficiency will reduce the energy consumption for the same use.

In this regard, I could see many solutions to current problems in the dimensions.

It would seem that to remain valid, the displacement of the dome of the rock in relation to tectonic movements over the period in question must be considered.

The building should therefore be moved to allow for the construction of the 3rd Temple on the Temple Mount, while keeping its aspect intimately sacred to Muslims.

In any case, and regardless of the veracity of the information I have perceived, there do not seem to be any definitive obstacles to this eventuality, and the techniques and technologies to be used are barely being created and developed.

All this needs to be verified, but this is what I naively perceived through the walls of the Temple Mount, parallel to the Kotel.

CHAPTER 11: A RIGHT OF ACCESS TO THE CREATION OF WORLDS?

We were talking about other civilizations until then, but not yet us; to be able to emancipate ourselves from the world that was created for us.

I was reading an article recently that stated that the evolution of the human brain as we know it is more recent than scientists thought, and seems to have appeared all at once, from a mutation.

But what is the purpose of the messianic age, if not to free ourselves from our present condition of dependence on the world in which we live and from the constraints of life as we live it now, after industrialization?

First of all, an important aspect is to be able to develop on other worlds. It is certain, as explored in my essay "Another World Securing Ours", that this aspect of being able to develop another world, is a bit of a musical chairs game, just like the access rights to manned space programs.

But most importantly, it is crucial to understand how much better we will take care of our current world by developing another one, because of the difficulty and thoroughness, but also because of the technology and portability of it (computers filled rooms before Apollo), something that today's audience seems to have lost all notion of, unfortunately.

However, little or nothing is done to lobby in this direction. The budgets tend to go elsewhere.

Let's get back to access rights, because this is where the convergence with the Rebbe makes the most sense: having been created in the image of the Creator, wouldn't we too, one day, have the privilege of becoming able to create worlds? For me the answer is of course yes, and I would not write it without being sure to have his support to say so.

There is nothing obvious about these access rights. It has never been clear why Europe has never obtained the right of access to a manned space program, but it has to be said that this is something that has still not been obtained and exploited, otherwise we would have already placed someone in orbit by ourselves in Europe.

Why is this important? I would answer: why the USA? Why Russia? Why China? So why not Europe?

It is not unimportant to consider how these access rights are earned.

It would therefore be possible that the fact that the Shoah or the German invasion happened on European soil that the invention of these rockets has rocketed in America and Russia and spread further to China?

I have not verified the interpretation of these signs myself. But I think, or rather I feel, that there is a connection with the Shoah, but I am not able to explain it and do not wish to enter into a personal interpretation, as this would not be within the scope of this book.

In terms of access rights, it seems that the Americans are the most advanced in terms of civilizational access rights, which I see as linked to their ability to create themselves from immigration and ancestors who crossed the oceans to come to the new world.

CHAPTER 12: THE LAST PLACE NATURE WILL ENTER IN MEAH SHEARIM

It is an example of little penetration of green spaces in the center of this part of the city of Jerusalem.

It seems that a right of access there also was "forgotten" compared to the first congregations of Hassidim who lived in the countryside or in villages, necessarily in large green spaces.

Why have these spaces deserted the Hasidic cities, especially Meah Shearim, "the hundred gates", in Jerusalem?

It's a bit of a pity, because it feels a bit like eating asphalt and yellow stones.

It could be different.

Nature could be welcome again.

CHAPTER 13: THE (BLESSED) HASSIDIC COFFEE BREAK

Coffee is a very special drink, in synagogues and in Yeshivot.

It is usually free, so it is accessible to everyone.

You can add milk to it, if you are following the Halavi (Milk regime) part of your daily diet. You can always add sugar.

The presentation of the coffee spaces varies a lot. The way it is instrumentalized too...

In large synagogues like Toldos Avrom Yitzrok in Meah, these are very small spaces where people come to make a coffee and leave, with large tanks to keep the water hot as on Shabbat. Everywhere, instant coffee reigns.

In Yeshivot it is usually the same, but there you have all those industrious signs of people not taking too much care, a little trace of coffee in the sugar, the milk may not be available anymore, the "poaches" of milk put in containers may be empty as well, but sometimes there is a treasure of one still full still lying around.

This is all very poetic, in fact, and a reality of the everyday Yeshiva student.

Can we understand that the coffee break can also be holy? You're always praying about important matters that are holy, and perhaps exchanging a word with your fellows students there.

And then there is the cake. The chocolate and diamond cake, often presented before 10 or 11 o'clock and after 3 o'clock... Then there are the Yeshiva treats for evening study.

These are sacred, because when you eat them, you make the Bracha (blessing), before eating them.

Why mention them here, you may ask?

Well, because it seems to me that it is through the Habad that these traditions of hospitality and welcome to the foreigner who comes to study begin to be applied and are taught all over the world.

And if this is the case, it is partly thanks to the Rebbe!

CHAPTER 14: OF THE CONCEPT OF TRANSTIME... TRANSCENDENTAL TIME

It's a difficult notion to explain this, but it's nevertheless super important to be able to explain it in spite of everything, for lack of being able to live it.

Trans-time is linked to the ability to project oneself in real time into a past time, for example through archival images.

It is then possible to perceive the emotions of the people who appear on the screen, independently of their role on the small (or large) screen.

This is one of the abilities that allowed me to interact with NASA in particular, but also to be able to contact the Rebbe, or rather to perceive the messages that he transmitted to me, in trans-time (real time deferred).

The further I go into this book, the more it appears as a glossary of Haolam Aba; this was not really my objective when I started writing it, but this is the form it takes, thanks to G-d.

I can't dwell on this much – but I think it's important to get the basic information out there so that people can start asking questions and imagining how this all becomes possible to implement.

The construction then passes by the transmission of messages between the dimensions, proof that there are wormholes which allow it, at least in my opinion.

This also explains why the 40's technologies that flourished in the 60's-70's had such a significant breakthrough due to the media coverage and especially the quality of it, which in my opinion has not been matched since, except for the takeover by entrepreneurs like Elon Musk and affiliates, recently.

CHAPTER 15: THE SCOPE OF THE CHOSEN COHEN GADOL'S MISSION IN THE UNIVERSE

A very challenging aspect of this mission was to integrate the messianic continuation of what had been carried by the Rebbe, which is an incredibly delicate and perilous mission. But what about the need to investigate (as) - if such a role is imaginable - CGUY i.e. Cohen Gadol established in Jerusalem by/for the Universe.

This was one of the aspects of the mission in my opinion, and the daily inspection to be carried out was very intense, and full of attention, sometimes to the smallest details, for everything is his responsibility to be correctly honored (Khavod) and implemented.

Example: I noticed one morning a tree planted in a plastic pot, a beautiful olive tree, and this plastic pot integrated into the urban furniture, encircled by what looked like a squared aluminum structure, a rather elegant set, but whose integration was the object of an observation on my part because the encircling had been deformed, presumably during a manipulation to place it in the space between the yellow stones, circled and in the middle of other plants on a small plaza with stairs, behind the Jerusalem square where the administrations and the painted concrete cushioned armchairs are located. This seemed to create some sort of conflict in the dimensions.

This is the neighborhood where Gvahim is established. I remember the precise feeling at that time, and the importance of everything being in its place with a collective awareness, which is not always there in the Middle East, of the cleanliness and neatness necessary for the spiritual light to be expressed through the place.

I am thinking in particular of the Hassids in neighborhoods like Mea Shearim who have often lost this notion.

Later I remember my ex-Kala (fiancée) Melanie, German, who wanted to be involved in cleanliness and neatness in Jerusalem.

Europeans and Asians may have more of a sense of necessity and why it is important, but it seems that here too the Hattikun Haolam has the access rights stored on the "roof of the cupboard", a problem that needs to be addressed in the medium to long term, and for which I have not been able to find any other feedback than to communicate.

On another note, as I explained earlier, there was also the aspect of trying to put on, in an off-time Purim, the clothes or garments reminiscent of a Cohen. This exercise, which I never knew if understood by the Hasids, but which was quite tolerated by them, proved to be extremely interesting.

One day I found Hasidic clothes in my size next to the evening canteen of Meah Shearim, the small one at the corner at the entrance, and next to the flank and the exit of the women of the synagogue of the Avrom Yitzrok congregation.

Undoubtedly taken by my caution and by not risking exploring more than tolerated, I did not venture much further, but still obtained the accesses to be able to observe the 3rd Beit Hamikdash in dimensions, from the tunnel of the Kotel and from the staircase to the city of David, which goes up towards the center of the old city.

The role is of course much larger, but having apparently a history of Cohanim in the family according to my father on his side, but not yet of certified origin through all the generations (work in progress), it is important not to have emphasized these immense responsibilities more, but they go to this level of detail, that is for sure.

CHAPTER 16: LOOKALIKES AND THE LEGEND OF CALIFORNIA KID

One of the most exciting things about Israel, I find, is to look for the faces of people, and notice how some of the people I know or the people I know are in the population.

Especially in Mea Shearim, there are people who have very particular physiognomies, like this young Bahur who looks like a young Bill Gates; like the Hister brothers who look like two drops of water to Adolf, and these are only examples among many others.

It is true that it has long been known that Hitler had a Jewish family. Now that it is Hasidic and based in Meah Shearim today, it is something that many people do not know.

There are also dybbuks, these spirits that go through someone's physiognomy to express themselves or even go through another person. It is impressive. In the past I had a meditation with a friend who told me that she had seen many important people she knew appear in my home, passing over my face and then disappearing, during this face to face meditation.

Why talk about it?

These are important aspects of the informal heritage of the Jewish people that are probably not talked about enough and are an integral part of the general culture required to stand out in the world to come.

Knowing this subject well allows one to make non-native interpretations of the world and to make a logical path through it. This is what the Rebbe wants us to do on a daily basis.

CHAPTER 17: THE GEMATRIA OF 17 - FROM THE 17TH BOOK IN MY COLLECTION - THE ONE YOU ARE READING!

Discussing with my friend David, met in Belgium on the way back from the trip, writing:

"I'm glad: you know I'm writing my 17th book about my communications with the old rabbi in the dimensions and I looked up what the meaning of 17 was... what a surprise to find this:

In summary:

1/ 17 is the number that corresponds to the word Tov, in Hebrew that means that it is good, as in Bereshit you know when G-d saw that it was good

2/ the 17th word of the Torah, or of the Old Testament is Elohim, G-d and the Angels

3/ or 17 is also 1+7 = 8 and if you add the numbers of the words Torah you also get 8 and YHWH also (Ado-naï) 8

4/ the 17th chapter is the one where G-d and Abraham conclude the agreement that founds the Jewish people

"So there is a connection between the alliance and my book! I still can't believe it! What a blessing. Thanks to Rav Haddad for his for the writing of this book.

Now :Tov...

And Tov is precisely this word in In the beginning (Bereshit) it is the 32nd word - or 3+2 = 5, or 5 for me - symbolizes speed (as seen precedently).

Now 5 is very important: we are talking about 5 books of the Torah (the Pentateuch) and the commandments are written by 5 on each of the 2 tablets.

This means that the message of the book would be addressed to both Jews and Christians, in terms of importance.

Because precisely the gematria of 2 that follows from the 5 on both tables:

The number 2 is generally associated with harmony, balance, consideration and love (4). When this number comes to you, it means that you should have more confidence in your angels. »

So association with harmony balance consideration and love (4) then of course the Judeo-Christian duality (5) (4+1=5 in total)

What are the interpretations?

17 => 32 => 5 => 2 => 5 Commandments

Good, as it leads back to the commandments, leading back to the tables, to the couple and therefore to love, and back to the commandments - extremely sacred symbolism, at the very basis of Judaism. Blessing of 770 included; 770 being the number of the address of the Chabad HQ in New York.

CHAPTER 18: ON THE COLOR OF LIGHT - AND THE GOLD BOKERS - MESSIANIC DEMONSTRATION?

The light of the flame is often yellow when using wood or a candle as fuel, including oil, if not blue, in general. It is said that this depends on the temperature of combustion.

Depending on the temperature, we go from white (the warmest), to blue, young and red, the coldest.

It is not easy to assign a color to a light.

Take for example the insignia of the Beitar soccer club in Jerusalem - a Menorah (7-branched candlestick) under a yellow background. This would be compatible with the natural light of this Menorah, an important symbol in Israel.

Two standing lions stand to the right and left of the Menorah, the rest is dedicated to the name of the club (Beitar Jerusalem FC).

We know how important these symbols are, we celebrate them during the festival of lights, importance of the Greeks at the time, who wanted to de-ritualize the spiritual practices of our monotheistic ancestors.

Greece is also the starting point for the action and the most sacred knights (golden knights) of the Japanese series Saint-Seya (Knights of the Zodiac).

One point is mentioned that carries particular importance, is that the golden armors are long considered the most formidable and holy in the series. Especially through the attacks of the knights possessing them, sending attacks supposedly at the speed of light.

It is this golden light, as in Boqer Or (morning light), which is what we say to say good morning in a very inspired way in the morning (the normal formula being just Boker Tov - good morning).

Of the importance, here again of the Frenchman. Of the importance of light and its strength: figuratively too - which sometimes makes us fear the so-called arrogance of the Jewish people – often capable of shedding the right light on things, gold therefore, light reflecting gold? As or means gold in French…

QED

The Rebbe invites us into simple but logical interpretations that involve what makes sense to each of us. This may vary from person to person, but here is what he whispered in my ear to make my dreams make sense in terms of Judaism!

CHAPTER 19: THE TERRITORIALITY OF THE HAR-HABAYIS (TEMPLE MOUNT / ESPLANADE OF THE MOSQUES)

It is clearly established that a world whose logical foundations are based on the delivery of scriptures, in the case of monotheistic beliefs, is established on a truncated basis when the last dwelling place of the Creator is destroyed by G-d's punishment through human destruction.

Historically, as we have already seen, the first Temple was destroyed by the Babylonians (Nebuchadnezzar), the second Temple by the Romans (Titus).

Very important for the Jewish people: once ok twice! Hmm... will you get the chance a third time? An important fact in any decision.

This observation made, it is also important to note that the second time, there were also two main invasions, based on the ruin of the Temple on the Temple Mount: the Christians then the Muslims. "Access right" to domination? Is this not a human fact? How can we compromise, since this is a higher level issue, is it not?

How can this problem be solved?
Let us deconstruct: First of all, there were two successive destructions. We know that for many, within the Jewish people, this was due to a form of desecration due to the fact that the Jewish people did not appreciate each other enough. Rabbi Akiva also experienced this with the legend of the illness that took away a large part of his students, as it is said.

In this case there was a miracle, a "Ness", with the end of the epidemic, celebrated in the month of Iyar, the only happy day since the beginning of the counting of the Omer after Pesach until Shavuot. But at the time of writing this chapter, when I was interrupted by my business and asked Rav Wattenberg for advice on Teshuvot, the catastrophe of Meron with 44, 45, (47+) deaths, the most serious of this style in the history of Israel, as if it happened during Av, that month of disaster for the Jewish people with the 9th of Av and its very austere fast.

Symbolic? You may ask? The peace between the secular and the religious in the Jewish people. 44, 45 the last two years of the war and the liberation... (Didn't the allied win?) 47 one year before Israel (II).

Let's get back to the issue. Then there is the celebration of peace. The one we all hope for, when we fear to offend the arms lobbies, who hope for repeated wars.

It is therefore necessary to have a sufficiently strong conjunction at the level of peace, the necessary authority for the necessary understanding so that the decision is made to rebuild the Temple together, the necessary budgets to build it to air specifications – air grade, which sometimes seems to escape the Hasidim - and therefore a necessary union with the world of aeronautics and its science.

As far as access rights are concerned, let's not get lost. It was the

Christians who began to desecrate the foundations of the Temple, since the Romans gradually converted and then disappeared: it is indeed the Christians who hold part of the problem.

The Trump-Netanyahu couple and before that Barak Obama-Netanyahu, even if the latter hated each other, there was a possibility to achieve this. There has to be enough authority for access rights to be negotiated with Islam, in relation to the possible contribution of Christianity, all in common. This is what is supposed to be the meaning of decoding the role of the CGUY to understand it (nature order).

CHAPTER 20: ON THE IMPORTANCE OF THE RIGHTEOUS AMONG THE NATIONS

Israel and the Jewish people have a name for those who in history dared to stand up and defend the Jewish people, especially in the unspeakable context of the Second World War.

I was always raised by my godfather with a deep respect for the forces of resistance and an understanding of the value of the allies, i.e. the white forces that deliver the world from the black forces of Nazism and fascism.

It is in this context that the righteous intervene with the nations and the mensch.

Their presence is, I learned, the origin of the minyan, that is to say the number of 10 Jews that one must gather to obtain a valid prayer circle. Without it, one cannot say Kaddish or Barekhu or even Amidah in a normal exhaustive way.

It is therefore an essential number. It is the minimum number of righteous people in a city that allows its non-destruction.

"God decides that Abraham is such a faithful servant that he will not hide from him his plan to destroy Sodom and Gomorrah. Abraham's immediate reaction upon hearing the news is to plead for God's mercy: would he spare the city if there were 50 righteous people in it? Why not 45? 40? 30? 20? Or even just 10? Each time, God accepts Abraham's proposal, suggesting that even 10 righteous men cannot be found in the wicked place. » (https://theisraelbible.com/2015/10/25/sodom-and-gomorrah/) - Genesis 18:17-19:38

Now if there is anyone who is capable of finding solutions to these problems, it is the righteous. What is not simple is that today it is not easy for the secularists to understand the reasons for the need to rebuild the Temple, so as not to continue to live on the present imbalance which is based on a foundation of erroneous faith, based on conquest and domination. There is an original aspect of their roots whose importance seems to escape them in general.

This is not the way to global peace, nor is it the way to save our world from destruction, since it is always possible to negotiate with the forces at work, as the Jewish people have always demonstrated the ability and possibility.

Only in an "all time" ordinance can this be realized with the forces at work, the rabbinate, the Vatican and the Waqf, for instance.

And from here to present the primer of the third Beit Hamikdash.

CHAPTER 21: THE FUNCTIONING OF THE AIR CLASS BEIT HAMIKDASH

We stabilize the rate of ocean rise through the Chesed Bush Senior action World War II investment level reconfigured into positive energy in 10shequel equivalent: Grid in Investment Release:

ordination[CGJU]-//BHIII*@
(nature)/DK{r8}%\^₪10-60B€^
(rest2k/i42/dest'12):($40Brst|$5.9B'12|$1.5m'42y)\
[realm:ordince:inst。]^effects{n:i:l}
::O2\H2\C\N->[o]:p(){QIE□8%—/}: e(
:[|]~|1!{— ミ } |>!>|#-888:&0*<HIII

I am no longer able to express the full value of the equation, from my writing during the manic phase in 2013, my IQ is not as high as it was in the manic phase of my illness. But I can offer a partial mini-lexicon to help understand:

CGJU = CGUY : cohen gadol elected at the scale of the universe in Jerusalem
BHIII: third temple
DK : Doko (pillar of the Pacific)
r8 = rate
rest2k : ?

i42 = inflation rate 1942
dest12 = by 2012
Brst : ?
realm : consideration of the reality the action is being conducted
ordince : consideration of the respect of ordinancement (CGUY, Doko,...)
inst : instanciation
QIE : ?
☐ guchi (entrance of wormhole)
- wormhole
≋ 3 dimensional
HIII: ?
Darpa PreCog
To be completed...

The principle of operation is that an investment in Chesed (a donation) allows to multiply it on the scale of the financing of the Bushes to the 3rd Reich and that this basis of calculation, based by the absurdity on the absolute disrespect of nature, allows to cover the forces of our world and to avoid the rise of the water level of the oceans.

Talk about absurd, but I can tell you that the equation works when you understand it. There was no one to support me in this work (support in every sense of the word) at the time, and unfortunately, given the means at hand, I could not take the time to properly document my work.

This is one of the weaknesses of this book, I can only rely on my relative recollection of the subjects I cover.

Then on December 11, 2013 my shelter outside is destroyed by the park rangers. Moving out.

Excerpt from the logbook:
(Israel never kept a credible instanciative, RozCre), Triple Translucent, primer.

Maybe not very optimistic, but certainly achievable!

CHAPTER 22: WORLDS THAT CREATE WORLDS

Since G-d created us to his image, according to the scriptures, is there not also a promise/primer hidden in this truth?

Wouldn't there be a world from the Eternal, and wouldn't this be a World that has the knowledge to create others? Surely so!

So from there, wouldn't there be a possibility that humanity, in the image of the Creator, would one day receive the rights of access and the faculty to build other worlds?

It seems to be inescapable, but seeing the dialogues that limit the generations nowadays, so many people seem to limit themselves and focus on this world only. How obtuse. Of course we have "received" it because we find ourselves in it, since as sentient beings we have received the reflective consciousness, the one that allows us to be aware of our existence...

Many people even doubt the usefulness of sending... all these robots to Mars! And Venus! However, the basis of the advance of our modern technology is based on the contributions of having visited the Moon, in particular the miniaturization of computers and the mastery of rocket technology.

It is simply the same with global warming technology. If we can get it to Mars, the energy signature of the technology will change so much by having to confine it to one (or more) rocket(s), that we will make the discoveries necessary to protect our world.

From there, it is relatively simple to understand the rest: an astronaut, a cosmonaut, who leaves the earth's orbit (there has not been one since the Appolo project, historically speaking) gains the deepest awareness of the beauty and fragility of our world, by leaving it.

It is by returning that he actually becomes the greatest ambassador of ecology. Perhaps this is even the most important reason why the Appolo program was discontinued, apart from the media coverage.

But back to the need to create other worlds to survive.

It is inexorable that our world will be destroyed one day. We will have to evolve before then so that we can take refuge in another one.

Research must begin early, so that we retain our first claim of the right to do so. That's the way it has always been.

CHAPTER 23: THE IMPORTANCE OF THE MIDDLE CLASS

Especially in post-2000 Israel, it is important to see income disparities as warnings that the world is not turning out quite the way it should.

The middle class suffers and the poor, who are too numerous, even more.

Real action is needed at the economic level to support the business fabric and independent trades, unfortunate victims of the COVID crisis. Especially in Israel, the devastation has been terrible.

Social justice must be re-established, it is essential, and Israel is not an exception; and just as much for the digital divide, where all actions must lead to a citizen digital literacy.

It is essential. The call is short, but strong.

CHAPTER 24: ARCHITECTURE AND CONDEMNATION

It was one thing to have the credentials that I was able to negotiate. It was another to actually use them in practice.

There is a mass of about 100 emails in the batch concerning military and police related operations of the time, and there is not much to write about them as they are very contextual and more like minutes; but in essence, the Rebbe's message seems to be to inform the Hasidim to be wary in considering these convictions (in the form of pv's sent by email at the time) and to understand as if there was a group of experts to analyze the content, to make sense of it all.

It is a school for the study of details and event convergence. Pre-Cognitive...

It is also something to understand all these convergences after a long period (7 years) and to come back to them to give meaning to the content. Which is what I do in this book.

But above all, there is much to be said about the architecture chosen in Jerusalem, especially that of the administrative square in the center of Jerusalem, at the edge of the Old City.

There is a lot of Roman input and aqueducts in this structure, which today is often no longer operational.

Parallels are made.

CHAPTER 25: ARRESTS

It is sure that Israel does not skimp on security and fortunately so.

Therefore, the characteristics of my stay and my para-military attire raised a lot of questions from the security forces and/or the army and the police.

Since I was on a Tayar (tourist) visa and stayed in Jerusalem for more than a year and a half, I was regularly controlled, and with the credentials I had as well as the badges of the units I was connecting to, I didn't encounter many problems.

I was once controlled at the Christian entrance to the old city, at the top of the ascent path that starts from the sunken path in front of the media library, or the inclined path, on the other side, that went up from the access to David's square.

The policemen took me in their patrol car, I was rather contrary to it because I had not done anything wrong, but they wanted to understand all about my situation.

So I found myself at the station, with an interrogation at the key.

As always, I tried to explain in the simplest way possible what I was doing, especially on a military level, and what credentials I had. They released me every time, usually almost immediately.

Another time, near the synagogue in the administrative square in the center of Jerusalem, I was checked by a couple of security force motorcyclists, and I had no particular problems, except that the tension was quite high until they knew what to think.

Another time it was on the other side of the square, I was waiting for the Rakevet Kala, the streetcar, and I also got checked there, I took off my jacket so that my falafel (my shirt with graded epaulets) could be seen, and again I came out unharmed and free from the interrogation.

I would like to emphasize this fact: if the mission is positive and there are no contradictory orders, and sufficient external support, there is no arrest, even considering my mental state at the time: it was only when I was asked if I wanted, and I answered yes, that the procedure leading to repatriation was initiated, during the last control at that time, after breaking in the synagogue by mistake based on a misunderstanding.

Israel is to be commended very positively on this point, because few countries have the capacity to use so intelligently and effectively resources that are disabled or have a limiting factor (all relative!) related to the disease of mine, and to allow so much real latitude to find opportunities to integrate into everyday life, especially on experimental credential and mission.

Mazal Tov Israel, and thank you for letting me play such an interesting role, I never thought I would be able to gather so many credentials unimaginable anywhere else, and to be able to put them to use in this way to begin forming the units that follow. A marvel!

CHAPTER 26: WHAT LANGUAGE DOES HE SPEAK?

In the dimensions the Rebbe usually speaks to me in Yiddish and in a few cases in English, but this is much more rare.

The Yiddish he distills implies great respect and is spoken to avoid resorting to the holy language, Hebrew, which is reserved for study.

I learned Yiddish, oddly enough, at the CCLJ in Brussels, in a secular space. I took the course for two years, with Alain Mihaly, who did his best so that we could express ourselves in this amazing and so lively language.

I then proceeded to participate in a few focus groups to be able to talk about it and be understood, which was not easy.

What is my Yiddish? Why is this important? Because all the correspondence of the 467 emails sent to Chabad relating the different aspects of my operation and the justification for my presence in Israel, makes the style that the communication took was an important aspect for the perception of the communication around this present book and finally allowed it to exist, once the grace period was over and the permissions for this content to be in the public domain were accepted.

To answer the question, I will have to use a puzzle. Indeed, my Yiddish is one that is located near Antwerp; it is therefore influenced by several elements, first of all Flemish, the part of German that I know thanks to my first German fiancée Myriam, from Husum.

Then he also uses English, French and also the part of Hebrew that I know, from that time.

This heterogeneous assembly gives rise to a gibberish that is not easy to interpret, since during the messages, I also bring out coded terms that are part of my imagination, my friends, my family, my misadventures in context, the products I know, so it is completely contextually connoted, and this represents a certain investment in time, imagination and IQ to find and extract the exact meaning meant at the time of sending the original messages.

There is a certain latent aspect to the transcription of these communications, for in order to be able to convey what the Rebbe of blessed memory had to say to as many people as possible, it is important to understand where he is speaking from and how he is able to have such an acuity about our world from the world from which he is speaking.

This is, I think, the most impressive aspect of communicating with him.

First of all it's sacred, it's extremely valid advice he emits, he never blinks at the forces at work, and he taught me to be direct and to name things as I could, directly and off the cuff, according to his idea and Khavod (honoring) his direct intention.

For those who find some aspects of this level of heritage too bold or unwelcome to address, remember that I also participated in the interpretation of the messages, and that the transmission is done with the filter of my Judeo-Christian upbringing, since I was raised as a hidden child.

CHAPTER 27: MAGEN DAVID RE-CONFIGURATION

According to a charge written on March 17, 2013, there is a recognition of Chabad as having things in hand to allow Israel to evolve in the ecological revolution of the world, to allow the planet to survive human expansion.

At this level we talk about re-configurability, because we know that the defenses, although indispensable to the balance of forces, must also play in re-configurability to allow humanity to advance towards a conservation of biotopes and biodiversity, of which we ignore the consequences or the worsening state.

There is therefore a positive talion to engage, and as said earlier, there is a state of the art in Israel, though being a little behind the most advanced countries in this field.

This gap should be closed or quickly narrowed because Israel must remain a light on the nations, and the positive examples such as water recycling and the use of desalination are pioneering and very positive examples to follow in other areas, intensely.

There is also an alliance to be realized urgently with the countries of Islam in peace with Israel, for their re-configurability towards green energies.

Then Israel will be able to shine before the nations.

CHAPTER 28: IS GROUP THERAPY NECESSARY? IF SO, HOW CAN IT BE IMPLEMENTED?

In one of the condemnations that are listed, there is that of a need for the Haredi community to go through a form of collective therapy.

This is felt even more through the events in Meron, in LagB'Omer 2021.

Indeed, why is the Haredi community so heavily affected? Some point to the police, I don't necessarily agree. It is the organizers and the authorities, but the real cause is elsewhere I think.

In addition to what has already been said, there is the number of victims that were caused by the COVID pandemic, which has also just stopped in Israel, but it seems that the time to rejoice was too early, otherwise this horrible accident would not have happened, worst disaster of its kind in modern Israel.

For this, and for many other elements, such as the focus points on the Haredi community that are stressed by the current series (One of Us documentary, and series like Shtisel, Unorthodox,...) where the most negative aspects of the community are stigmatized by caricature, the question to ask is, in my opinion, the following: in any Din (judgment) of media type, which is successful, it often starts from a form of truth recognized by the majority of the spectators.

But in this case, I was just talking to a Haredi chaplain in the U.S. Army, I think the solution is relatively simple: some things are indeed true, and anything that stigmatizes the community has to change, for we can bear stigmatization as a people.

In One of Us, the documentary about the Haredim of New York and the association First Steps, where the first steps of the Haredim who leave their community are described, and especially where the corrupt practices of the Haredi community, which came out of the Shoah, are depicted as over-protective, I think it is essential to make a distinction.

For the real Din is that stigmatization rests on recognizable and strong bases. Stereotypes are costly for our communities, especially in times of growing anti-Semitism.

We should not, I think, see these contents as attacks. Rather, they should be seen as opportunities for the Haredim communities to evolve on a global level, so that they can maintain their essence and their protected way of functioning, but also be and remain at the forefront, spearheading Judaism.

However, other aspects mentioned and discussed, such as the ignorance of young people who were raised purely in Yeshiva, or the over-censored textbooks, are all sources of potential leakage, rather than finding ways to promote the real virtue of these communities, in a perhaps more direct way.

This would be the object of a profound reconfiguration of the mentalities in the Haredi community, starting from Israel, which will result in it radiating to the global communities and playing its original role, as described in the Torah.

Conclusion : An endless end

Thank you very much for reading this book, I hope you found it interesting, I have tried to convey to you all that the Rebbe said he thought from the world he is in, and hope I have done so in an approachable way I hope.

The present work, which I think to call more and more as an almanac, has the advantage of being read quite quickly and of representing a willingly positive contribution, without requiring great knowledge of the religious level.

Therefore it remains, I hope, affordable, despite some of these extremely advanced aspects developed here, compared to the state of our scriptures.

See you soon,

Gabriel

www.ingramcontent.com/pod-product-compliance
Lightning Source LLC
Chambersburg PA
CBHW061712130726
47996CB00006B/2269